P9-EDS-259

Let's Play Tag!

📖 Read the Page

▶ Read the Story

🔄 Repeat

⏹ Stop

⭐ Game

⭐ Level 1   ⭐⭐ Level 2   ⭐⭐⭐ Level 3

💻

TO USE THIS BOOK WITH THE TAG™ READER you must download audio from the LeapFrog Connect application. The LeapFrog Connect application can be installed from the CD provided with your Tag Reader or at leapfrog.com/tag

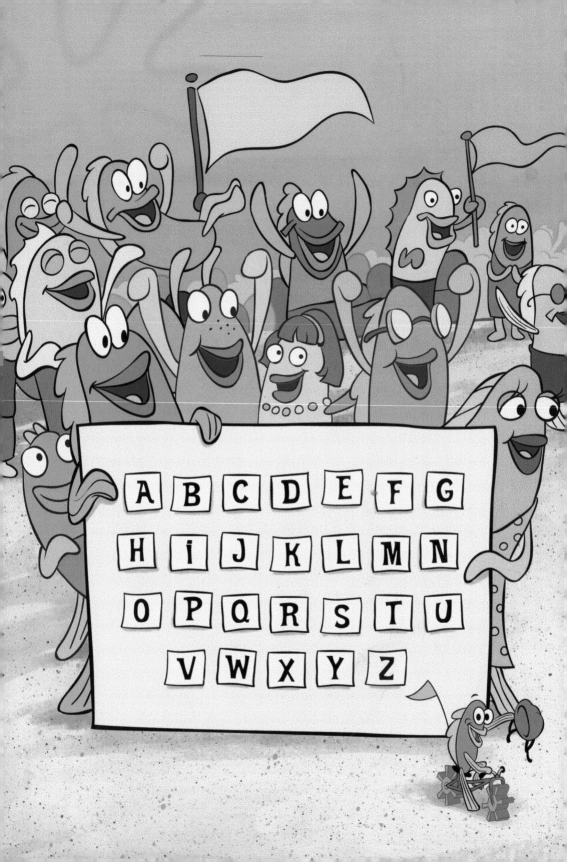

The TOUR de BIKINI BOTTOM

written by Scott Sonneborn
illustrated by Warner McGee

The Tour de Bikini Bottom was the biggest bike race in town.

"Good luck, Squidward!" said SpongeBob.

"I don't need luck," said Squidward.

"I ride my bicycle every day," bragged Squidward. "I would be shocked if I didn't win."

But Squidward wasn't winning.
"I can't believe it," said Squidward sadly.

SpongeBob felt bad. "Squidward really
wants to win," SpongeBob said to Patrick.
"We should help him."

"What if we give him this Krabby Patty?" asked Patrick. "Will that help Squidward win?"

"It just might!" said SpongeBob.

"That's too bad," said Patrick. "Because I wanted to eat it."

SpongeBob tried to give the Krabby Patty to Squidward.

"What are you doing?" cried Squidward. "I can't see where I'm going with a Krabby Patty in my face!"

Squidward ran off the road and hit a rock. He flew into the air and landed in Goo Lagoon.

"That didn't help Squidward," said Patrick.

"We just have to keep trying," said SpongeBob.

So SpongeBob and Patrick tried something different.

And then something else.

And then a different something else.

But after everything they did,
Squidward was still in last place.

Then Patrick had an idea. "If trying to help Squidward win is making him lose," said Patrick, "maybe if we try to make him lose, it will help him win!"

"I am glad I have a smart friend like you, Patrick!" said SpongeBob.

There was a sign on the road. It told the riders which way to go. SpongeBob turned it around.

Squidward saw the
sign and went the
wrong way.

Race

FINISH

"Yaaarrrggghhh!"
yelled Squidward,
as he flew off the mountain.

"Can you hear what Squidward
is saying?" asked SpongeBob.

"I think he's trying to thank us,"
said Patrick.

FiNiSH

The other riders were almost at the finish line when Squidward fell right on top of them!

The race was over. Squidward won by
a nose!

"I did it!" said Squidward.

"We did it!" said SpongeBob and Patrick.

The End.

bit

dim

fin

hid

kit

rip

Silent e Cheer!

bite

dime

fine

hide

kite

ripe

19

wheel

weed

beam

creek

street

seat

tree

bean

queen

meal

beet

PAST	PRESENT
honked	honking
stomped	stomping
twirled	twirling
wiggled	wiggling
screamed	screaming
yodeled	yodeling
drooled	drooling
burped	burping
gargled	gargling

"Last year, Squidward _____ in the Tour de Bikini Bottom. He barely _____ into last place! So a month before this year's race, Squidward trained. Every day he _____ for twenty minutes and _____ a healthy bowl of Kelpo cereal.

Right now I am _____ with this year's big winner, Squidward Tentacles! Just this minute Squidward is _____ at his fans. Squidward, do you have anything to say?"

"I did it all by myself!"

handlebar

tour

pump

lock

horn

contest

speed

team

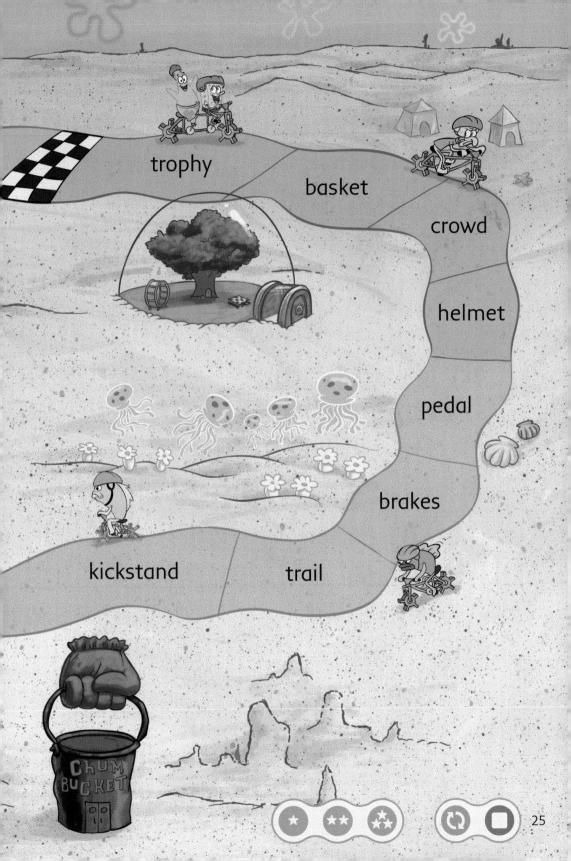

trophy

basket

crowd

helmet

pedal

brakes

kickstand

trail

CHUM BUCKET